We for Knowing How to Have *Fun!*

Celebrating the blessings of
friendship, laughter & special times

Inspired by Faith

We have a Gift...for Knowing How to Have Fun!
ISBN 978-0-9859685-5-7

Published by Product Concept Mfg., Inc.
2175 N. Academy Circle #200, Colorado Springs, CO 80909

©2012 Product Concept Mfg., Inc. All rights reserved.

Written and Compiled by Vicki J. Kuyper
in association with Product Concept Mfg., Inc.

All scripture quotations are from the King James version
of the Bible unless otherwise noted.

Scriptures taken from the Holy Bible,
New International Version®, NIV®.
Copyright © 1973, 1978, 1984 by Biblica, Inc.™
Used by permission of Zondervan.
All rights reserved worldwide.
www.zondervan.com

Sayings not having a credit listed are contributed by writers
for Product Concept Mfg., Inc. or in a rare case,
the author is unknown.

We have a Gift...
for Knowing
How to
Have *Fun!*

*Of all the things which wisdom acquires to
produce the blessedness of the complete life
far the greatest is the possession of Friendship.*

Epicurus

Sure, we can have *fun*
when we're alone. We can read a book,
watch TV, bake a batch of brownies…
eat a batch of brownies all by ourselves.
But when those we love are near,
joy just seems to multiply. Thank you
for being the kind of person who makes
everything better just by being there.
You add so much love—and laughter—
to my life!

*A*mong those whom I like,
      I can find no
common denominator;
      but among those whom I love,
I can: all of them
      make me laugh.

W. H. Auden

The most wasted day of all
      is that on which we have
            not laughed.
Sébastien Roch Nicolas Chamfort

You Can Call on Me

Laura's car was totally unreliable.
But Laura's friend, Kelly, wasn't.
So when Laura's car broke down,
she called on Kelly.
"So, what's gone out this time?" Kelly asked.
"The brakes," Laura replied.
"Where are you?" Kelly asked.
"The pharmacy," Laura responded.
"And where's the car?" Kelly asked.
Laura sighed, "In here with me."

Just For Fun!

Invite everyone over to your house for a "virtual" pool party. Work together to secure a big, blue piece of plastic in your backyard. Then, when people see satellite images of your home online, they'll think you have a swimming pool!

Women Worth Hanging Out With...

- *assure you that you have an hourglass figure, even when the sands of time begin to shift.*

- *don't bat an eye when you order a side of chocolate chips with your salad.*

- *may witness you making a fool of yourself, yet don't believe it's a permanent condition.*

*T*he kitchen,
the coziest place that I know:
The kettle is singing,
the stove is aglow,
And there in the twilight,
how jolly to see
The cocoa and animals
waiting for me.

Christopher Morley

True Confessions

"My husband tried to cook while I was away on my business trip," Jean told her friend over lunch at their favorite restaurant.
"So, how did it go?" Tami asked.
"Not so well," Jean confided.
"He said every recipe he tried was so demanding, he never got past the first line."
"What do you mean?" said Tami.
"They all started with, 'Take a clean dish…'"

I know not whether
our names will
be immortal;
I am sure our
friendship will.

Walter Savage Landor

Friendship is a strong and habitual
inclination in two persons to promote
the good and happiness of one another.

Eustace Budgell

From quiet homes
and first beginning,
Out to the undiscovered ends,
There's nothing worth
the wear of winning,
But laughter and
the love of friends.

Hilaire Belloc

Definition of FRIEND:

a) somebody who has a close personal relationship of mutual affection and trust with another

b) YOU!

Definition of FUN:

a) a time or feeling of enjoyment or amusement

b) an activity that provides enjoyment or amusement

c) playful joking

d) any time spent or activity shared with YOU!

The Family Tree of Friendship

Friends come in all shapes and sizes, ages and bloodlines. Sometimes, the roots of friendship begin at birth. Mothers, sisters, daughters…we're often blessed by being born, or adopted, into a family of lifelong friends.

Other friends begin as strangers. A chance meeting, a mutual acquaintance, a shared interest or casual conversation can all herald a new addition to our chosen family— the circle of friends that complete our lives by filling our hearts with joy.

Whether related by blood or experience, chosen by us or chosen first by God, it's in the company of these amazing women that we have the privilege to grow and grieve, live and learn, laugh and love.

Secret to a Happy Life:

Treat your friends like family
and your family like friends!

Just For Fun!

Invite your friends over for a Baby Face party. Have each person bring a photo of themselves as an infant. Have them place the pics in a bowl without showing them to anyone. Then, line the photos up on a table. Give each person paper and a pencil. Numbering the photos according to how they are lined up, have each person guess which photo matches which guest. Award the winner a baby bottle filled with something sweet, like jelly beans or individually wrapped chocolates.

*Y*ou can discover
more about a person
in an hour of play
than in a year
of conversation.

Plato

How many things,
which for our own sake
we should never do,
do we perform for the
sake of our friends.

Cicero

*O*h, the comfort—
　　The inexpressible comfort
of feeling safe with a person—
Having neither to weigh thoughts,
　　Nor measure words,
　　　　but pouring them
All right out just as they are—
　　Chaff and grain together—

Certain that a faithful hand will
Take and sift them,
Keep what is worth keeping,
and with the breath of kindness
Blow the rest away.

Dinah Maria Mulock Craik

*G*ood friends often finish
each other's sentences.
Really good friends help
finish each other's dessert.

It isn't so much what's
on the table that matters,
as what's on the chairs.

W. S. Gilbert

Phone call between two long-time friends:

When people spend a lot of time together, they may begin to think alike—and even finish each other's sentences.

"Hey…"
"Lunch?"
"Love to! Where?"
"That place with those sesame thingees?"
"You mean the one with the brass doodads on the table?"
"Yeah, where we last ran into what's her name."
"Perfect! Fifteen minutes?"
"See ya there!"

Just For Laughs!

*What did the green grape say
to the purple grape?*

… "Breathe! Breathe!!!!!"

*F*ortify yourself with a flock of friends! You can select them at random, write to one, dine with one, visit one, or take your problems to one. There is always at least one who will understand, inspire, and give you the lift you may need at the time.

George Matthew Adams

Open House

We just shake hands at meeting
With many that come nigh;
We nod the head in greeting
To many that go by.

But welcome through the gateway
     Our few old friends and true;
Then hearts leap up and straightaway
     There's open house for you,—
Old friends, there's open house for you!

Gerald Massey

Keeping It All in the Family

A daughter goes to visit her aging mother in the rest home. As she's waiting for her mother to wake up from her afternoon nap, she notices a bowl of peanuts beside her mother's bed and helps herself to one. As time passes, and her mother continues to sleep, the daughter polishes off the entire bowl.

When her mother wakes up the daughter says apologetically, "Mom! I'm so sorry, but it looks like I finished off all your peanuts."

"That's okay, honey," her Mom replies.

"Without my teeth, all I can do is suck the chocolate off and then spit them back in the bowl anyway."

Time Together

We're like two clocks keeping time, side-by-side. We know what makes each other tick—and, wow, can we "talk." We can unwind, charge each other's batteries or even sound an alarm in the other's presence, all while feeling perfectly comfortable displaying our true face.

We make time for one another, regardless of how crazy our schedules may be. And every hour, minute or second we share in each other's company is always time well spent.

*O*nce in an age,
   God sends to some of us
a friend who loves in us…
   not the person we are,
but the angel we may be.

Harriet Beecher Stowe

Just For Fun!

Head to a pet store with a friend. Pick out your dream pet (In your mind! No cash, commitment or clean up involved!). Then share with each other what you'd name your pet and why you chose the one you did. Chat about past pets and whether you'd consider them friend or foe today.

In times of joy,
we all wished we
possessed a tail we
could wag.

W. H. Auden

The true test of friendship
is to be able to sit or walk with
a friend for an hour in perfect
silence without wearying of
one another's company.

Dinah Maria Mulock Craik

Angels On Call

Those we love are angels in disguise. They ring us up for no reason—just to say, "Halo." If we need help anytime, anywhere, they're always ready to wing it. Their smile never fails to lift our spirits and provide us with a bit of heaven here on earth.

*T*t is my joy in life to find
　　At every turning of the road
The strong arms of a comrade kind
　To help me onward with my load;
And since I have no gold to give,
　And love alone must make amends,
　　My only prayer is, while I live—
God make me worthy of my friends.

F. D. Sherman

Ralph Waldo Emerson
On Friendship

We cannot part with our friends.
We cannot let our angels go.

Happy is the house that shelters a friend.

A friend is a person with whom I may be
sincere. Before him, I may think aloud.

The only way to have a friend is to be one.

Just For Laughs!

Ann's four-year-old son was thumbing through the big family Bible on the coffee table. Out fell a maple leaf Ann had placed between the pages to dry, planning to use it later in a fall flower arrangement.

"Look Mom," her son said, his eyes wide open in wonder. "I think it's Adam's suit!"

Good Friends
Don't Count

...how many trips you make
to the buffet table.
...the birthday candles on your cake.
...the number of times you've lost the
same five pounds.
...the favors they do for you.
...the mistakes you've made.

Above all, let us never forget that an act of goodness is in itself an act of happiness. It is the flower of a long, inner life of joy and contentment; it tells of peaceful hours and days on the sunniest heights of our soul.

Maurice Maeterlinck

A friend is a present
you give yourself.

Robert Louis Stevenson

Friendship is like a bank account;
you cannot continue to draw
on it without making deposits.

Samuel Butler

A friend loveth at all times.

Proverbs 17:17

A True Treasure

It's been said that man's best friend
*   is of canine persuasion,*
While women prefer diamonds
*   as their friends for all occasions.*
All I know is when it comes to friends
*   this much holds true:*
I found a perfect, priceless gem
*   the day that I met you.*

*   Vicki J. Kuyper*

You Could Use a Friend When...

Linda absent-mindedly grabbed her husband's glasses, instead of her own, as she hurriedly left for work one morning. Though the prescription was close, it was not close enough. Linda was only a few minutes from home when she was pulled over by a state trooper.

"M'am, is there a reason why you were weaving all over the road?" he asked.

"Officer, thank goodness you're here!" Linda said, visibly relieved. "I almost had an accident! I looked up and there was a tree right in front of me! I swerved to the *left and there was another tree right in front of me. Then I swerved right and there was STILL a tree right in front of me!"*

"M'am," the officer responded, "that's your air freshener."

Just For Fun!

Invite friends over for Buddies' Brownie Night. Beforehand, write wishes, prayers, compliments or quotes on small pieces of paper. (For example: "For all who see it, your smile brightens the day…Shine on!" or "May today be as beautiful of a blessing as the gift of your friendship is to others.")

Attach one end of each wish to the end of a toothpick with a piece of tape. Wrap the remaining paper tightly around the toothpick. Stick each toothpick in a brownie. Have each guest choose a brownie and then read their special message aloud.

The Perfect Square Meal:
a box of chocolates.

The 12-Step Chocoholic Program:
Never be twelve steps away from chocolate.

Words of Wisdom:
Nuts just take up space where chocolate should be.

A Wish Come True

A man found a bottle on the beach.
He opened it and out popped a genie
who gave the man three wishes. The man
wished for a million dollars and POOF!
A million dollars in cash appeared. Then
he wished for a convertible and POOF!
There was a red convertible parked on
the beach. Then, he wished he could be
irresistible to all women… and POOF!
He turned into a box of chocolates.

*A*gainst the assault
of laughter,
nothing can stand.

Mark Twain

What joy is better than
the news of friends?

Robert Browning

A feast is made for laughter.

Ecclesiastes 10:19

*S*mall service is true
service while it lasts.
Of humblest friends,
bright creature scorn not one!
The daisy, by the shadow
that it casts,
Protects the lingering
dew-drop from the sun.

William Wordsworth

Just For Laughs!

Mother to her daughter: Hey, there were two cakes in my pantry this morning. Now there's only one. Do you have any idea what happened?

Daughter: I guess it was so dark I didn't see the second one.

Sure Signs That You May Not Classify Exercise As "Fun"

You consider a bag of chips mandatory equipment when doing crunches.

Your morning exercise routine consists of: Up—1, 2, 3. Down—1, 2, 3. Then, the other eyelid…

You use candy wrappers as bookmarks.

*The closest you come to running "laps"
is eating in a revolving restaurant.*

*When told to touch your toes, you explain
you don't have that kind of relationship
and ask if it's okay to just wave.*

*You consider running late, pushing your
luck, jumping to conclusions and carrying
things too far all valid forms of exercise.*

In friendship we find
nothing false or insincere;
everything is straightforward,
and springs from the heart.

Cicero

The supreme happiness of life
is the conviction of being loved
for yourself, or, more correctly,
being loved in spite of yourself.

Victor Hugo

A Friendly Request

Pam wanted her good friend, Jean, to enroll with her in a yoga class.

"Absolutely not!" Jean exclaimed. "I tried that once!"

"What happened?" Pam asked.

"I twisted, hopped, jumped, stretched and pulled," Jean replied. "And by the time I got my yoga pants on the class was over!"

*W*e dare not trust
our wit for making
our house pleasant
to our friend,
so we buy ice cream.

Ralph Waldo Emerson

One song leads to another,
One friend to another friend,
So I'll travel along
With a friend and a song…

Wilfrid Wilson Gibson

*F*ather of all mankind,
  make the roof of my house
wide enough for all opinions,
  oil the door of my house
    so it opens easily
      to friend and stranger
and set such a table
      in my house that
  my whole family may speak
      kindly and freely around it.

Hawaiian Prayer

Just For Fun!

Always keep several Get
Well cards on the mantle
or kitchen counter. That
way, if unexpected guests
arrive they'll think you've
been sick and unable to
clean the house.

It was such a
lovely day I thought it
a pity to get up.

William Somerset Maugham

It is better to wear out than to rust out.

Saying

A day for toil, an hour for sport.
But for a friend is life too short.

Ralph Waldo Emerson

For new, and new,
and ever-new,
The golden bud
within the blue;
And every morning
seems to say:
"There's something
happy on the way..."

Henry Van Dyke

*T*here is no such thing
in anyone's life as
an unimportant day.

Alexander Woollcott

Life must be lived
and curiosity kept alive.

Eleanor Roosevelt

Happiness lies in the joy
of achievement and the thrill
of creative effort.

Franklin D. Roosevelt

Highway High Jinks

Joan had been driving along the highway for several hours. When she saw the sign, "Rest Area Next Exit," she immediately flipped on her turn signal. After parking the car, she hurried into the nearby restroom.

Joan had just sat down in the stall when the woman in the stall next to her decided to strike up a conversation. "Hi! How are you?" the stranger asked.

Thinking perhaps the woman was just trying to be friendly, Joan responded, "Fine."

But the woman continued. "So, what are you up to these days?"

"Uh, traveling, like you…" Joan answered, feeling more than a little self-conscious. Then, there was silence. Joan figured the overly-friendly inquiry had come to an end.

Then, the woman asked abruptly, "Hey, can I come over?"

Joan started to panic. She was ready to hastily pull herself together and race back to the car when she heard the woman say, "Listen, I'll have to call you back. There's a crazy woman in the next stall who keeps trying to talk to me!"

Ay, there are some
good things in life,
That fall not away
with the rest.
And, of all best
things upon earth,
I hold that a faithful
friend is the best.

Owen Meredith

*M*ake yourself at home…
Clean my kitchen!

Best friend,
my well-spring in the wilderness!

George Eliot

Just For Laughs!

The minute little Janey got home from school she excitedly told her mother, "Today in class we learned how to make babies!"

Trying to keep her cool, her mother responded, "That's interesting, honey. How do you do that?"

Janey said confidently, "Change the 'y' to 'i' and add 'es.'"

*L*augh and the world laughs with you. Cry and you're forced to dig out that used fast food napkin at the bottom of your purse.

If the while I think on thee,
dear friend,
All losses are restored
and sorrows end.

William Shakespeare

*T*oday a new sun rises
for me; everything lives,
everything is animated,
everything seems to
speak to me of my passion,
everything invites
me to cherish it.

Anne de Lenclos

May you live all
the days of your life.
Jonathan Swift

Twenty years from
now you will be more
disappointed by the things
you didn't do than by
the ones you did do.
So throw off the bowlines!
Sail away from the safe harbor.
Catch the trade winds in your sails.
Explore. Dream. Discover!

Mark Twain

Signs that your CLOSEST friend may be caffeine...

- You have a picture of your coffee mug on your coffee mug.

- Every year, the country of Columbia sends you a Christmas card.

- You get a speeding ticket even when you're parked.

- You don't even wait for the water to boil when making a cup of instant.

- You forget to unwrap candy bars before eating them.

- You answer the door before people knock.

*C*offee: Induces wit.

Gustave Flaubert

I have measured out
my life with coffee spoons.
T. S. Eliot

Without my morning coffee
I'm just like a dried up
piece of roast goat.

Johann Sebastian Bach

DEJA BREW:

the feeling you're drinking
from the same pot of coffee
you did yesterday.

LATTE:

an Italian word meaning,
"You paid how much for that?"

Friends Are Like Coffee

You're smooth under pressure
And strong if I need it.
Any expectation?
You're sure to exceed it.
You make me feel confident,
Joyful and whole.
Yes, a good friend is like
Caffeine for my soul!

Vicki J. Kuyper

Putting the Pieces Together

Edna was Lucille's best friend at the rest home. So when Edna asked for help with a jigsaw puzzle, Lucille immediately sat down, ready to get to work.

Edna explained, "It's a really tough puzzle and I can't even figure out how to start."

"Well, Edna," said Lucille patiently, "what's the picture supposed to look like when you're finished?"

"A rooster," Edna said.

Lucille took a look at the box and then the puzzle pieces. Then she gently put her hand on her friend's shoulder.

"Relax, Edna," Lucille said. "I'll go get us each a nice cup of tea. Then I'll help you put all the corn flakes back in the box."

*E*ncourage one another
and build each other up,
just as in fact you are doing.

1 Thessalonians 5:11 NIV

I am still determined to be
cheerful and happy in whatever
situation I may be, for I have also
learned from experience, that the greater
part of our happiness or
misery depends on our dispositions
and not our circumstance.

Martha Washington

You and your circle of friends know you're getting older when…

- the gleam in your eye is from the sun hitting your bifocals.

- you turn off the lights early for economic rather than romantic reasons.

- you accidentally enter your password on the microwave.

- you wake up looking like your driver's license photo.

- you try to straighten out the wrinkles in your socks and discover you aren't wearing any.

As gold more splendid
from the fire appears,
Thus friendship brightens
by the length of years.

Thomas Carlyle

Everyone must have felt
that a cheerful friend is
like a sunny day,
which sheds its brightness
on all around.

John Lubbock

Fair Game

  You know you and the women you love are getting older when you come home from the county fair feeling sore all over—and all you've ridden is the massage chair.

Just For Fun!

Invite friends over for appetizers and conversation—BUT tape a 3 x 5 card under the table by each place setting. Beforehand, write an off-beat random phrase on each card, such as "'Syncope' means 'to faint,'" "In real life, I'm a zombie," or "Have you ever cooked with ostrich eggs?"

Instruct guests to read their cards silently before the party gets rolling and then try to work their phrase into the conversation. The goal is to guess what "phrase" each guest is trying to sneak in. Anyone who's phrase slips by undetected gets a prize.

Time you enjoyed wasting
is not wasted time.

T. S. Eliot

We must laugh and we must sing,
We are blest by everything,
Everything we look upon is blest.
William Butler Yeats

We cannot tell the precise
moment when friendship
is formed. As in filling a
vessel drop by drop, there is
at last a drop which
makes it run over;
so in a series of kindnesses
there is at last one which
makes the heart run over.

James Boswell

A kind heart is
a fountain of gladness,
making everything in its
vicinity freshen into smiles.

Washington Irving

Without wearing any mask
we are conscious of,
we have a special face
for each friend.

Oliver Wendell Holmes

Friendship Time Line

At 15 you and your friends decide to eat at the burger joint next to the "nice restaurant" because you only have $4.53 combined between the four of you—and that cute boy in history class works there.

At 25, your same group of friends meets at the "nice restaurant," because it has free appetizers and stays open late.

At 35, you meet there because it's close to the gym.

At 45…because they have low-fat options on the menu.

At 55…because the lighting is bright enough to read the menu.

At 65…because they have an early bird special.

At 75…because it's handicap accessible and the food isn't too spicy.

At 85…because none of you can remember having eaten there before.

*U*se what talents
you possess. The woods
would be very silent if
no birds sang there
except those that sang best.

Henry Van Dyke

Give what you have.
To someone it may be better
than you dare to think.

Henry Wadsworth Longfellow

Behold, I do not give lectures
or a little charity,
When I give, I give myself.

Walt Whitman

*J*ust being in your company
makes me believe I'm on vacation.
You turn even the smallest joy
into full-blown celebration.
You act as though loving others well
is your personal vocation.
That's why you're more
than just a friend—
You're my inspiration!

Vicki J. Kuyper

The real voyage of
discovery consists not
in seeking new landscapes
but in having new eyes.

Marcel Proust

The body travels more
easily than the mind, and until we
have limbered up our imagination,
we continue to think as though
we had stayed home. We have not
really budged a step until we take up
residence in someone
else's point of view.

John Erskine

*T*he best thing we
can find in our travels
is an honest friend.
He is a fortunate
voyager who finds many.

Robert Louis Stevenson

Happiness is essentially a state
of going somewhere, wholeheartedly,
one directionally,
without regret or reservation.

William H. Sheldon

Voyage, travel and change
of place impart vigor.

Seneca

Just For Laughs!

Did you hear about the cowgirl who wore paper pants, a paper shirt, paper boots and a paper hat?

The sheriff arrested her for rustling.

*L*aughter is the
sun that drives winter
from the human face.

Victor Hugo

The true atmosphere
of friendship is a sunny one.
Griefs and disappointments
do not thrive in its clear,
healthy light.

Randolph Bourne

My Friends Rock

Before I lay me down to sleep,
I pray, dear Lord, my friends you'll keep
Happy, healthy and full of laughter,
From this day forward until long after
Our hair turns gray or white or blue
And every day all that we do
Is sit around and reminisce
About good times, good friends...
such bliss!
'Cuz though we can't turn back the clock
My friends and I will always ROCK!

There is nothing more
special than a good friend—
Except a good friend who grows
to be an old friend.

Reality Check

"So, how did your annual physical go?" Sarah asked her friend, Susan.

"Horrible!" Susan said. "The nurse asked how much I weighed and I said, '135.' Then she put me on the scale and it said I weighed 180! Then the nurse asked for my height. I said, 'Five feet four inches.' She said, 'I only measure 5' 2".' Next she took my blood pressure and said it was really high. That's when I lost it!"

"What did you do?" Sarah asked.

"I screamed, 'Of course it's high! When I came in here I was like a fairy princess, tall and slender—now you're telling me I'm one of the seven dwarves!'"

*F*riendship is never
established as an understood
relation. It is a miracle which
requires constant proofs.
It is an exercise of the
purest imagination and
of the rarest faith…
The language of Friendship
is not words, but meanings.
It is an intelligence
above language.

Henry David Thoreau

*I*t's never too late
to be what you
might have been.

George Eliot

Treat your friends as
you do your pictures,
and place them in
their best light.

Jennie Jerome Churchill

My best friend is the one
who brings out the best in me.

Henry Ford

*B*lest be the tie that binds
Our hearts in Christian love;
The fellowship of kindred minds
Is like to that above.

John Fawcett

Just For Fun!

Purchase inexpensive plastic kazoos. Then gather your friends together for a musical extravaganza. Write the names of songs everyone will know on slips of paper. They could be contemporary, songs from your high school days, timeless classics, TV show themes, patriotic tunes, Broadway musical favorites or any combination. Have each person pick a slip of paper out of a bowl and then try to play the selection on a kazoo. See how long it takes others to name the tune. Guaranteed to jog your memory and tickle your funny bone!

*I*t is a splendid
habit to laugh inwardly
at yourself.

Henri de Tourville

Laughter is not at all
a bad beginning for a friendship…

Oscar Wilde

$\mathcal{I}$'d like to be the sort of friend
you have been to me.
I'd like to be the help that you've
been always glad to be.
I'd like to mean as much to you
each minute of the day,
As you have meant,
old friend of mine,
to me along the way.

Edgar A. Guest

Wanted:
One Terrific Friend

We all have unwritten job descriptions for our friends. Not only do we expect them to be fun to hang out with, we often rely on them to be our most candid sounding boards. At any given moment, we expect them to fill the role of mentor, teacher, mother, sister, stylist, financial planner, coach, therapist or cheerleader.

In the midst of all those expectations, let's not forget to also expect them to be human. We all fail from time to time—us, and our friends. Let's extend to each other the grace to fail, as well as fly. That's what true love, and friendship, is all about.

Everyone Makes Mistakes... Even Teachers

Having been laid off from her teaching position several months earlier, Sophia was certain she'd have no trouble finding a new job. She had experience, great references, a solid education and a willingness to move anywhere—even far away from her wonderful circle of friends.

Sophia carefully crafted a cover letter and attached a copy of her current resume. Then she emailed it to over two-dozen prospective employers.

A week went by. Then two. There was no response to her email. Sophia began to get anxious about not having received a single request for an interview. Perhaps finding a job was going to be much more difficult than she'd first believed.

Finally, one morning she saw a reply in her email in-box. Anxiously, she clicked to open it. The email read:

Dear Ms. Greene,
Your resume was not attached as stated. However, I would like to thank you for the wonderful Fettuccine Alfredo recipe.

Sincerely,
Janet Pierce
Principal, Perkins Middle School

Madame de Staël is
such a good friend,
she would throw all
her aquaintances in the water
for the pleasure of
fishing them out again.

Charles Maurice de Talleyrand

Friendship is a word
the very sight of which in print
makes the heart warm.

Augustine Birrell

I want a warm and faithful friend
　　To cheer the adverse hour;
Who ne'er to flatter will descend,
　　Nor bend the knee to power,—
A friend to chide me when I'm wrong,
　　My inmost soul to see;
And that my friendship prove as strong
　　For him as his for me.

John Quincy Adams

Food For Thought...

— If a pig loses it's voice, is it disgruntled?
— Do Roman paramedics refer to IV's as 4's?
— When cheese gets its picture taken,
  what does it say?
— If lawyers can be disbarred, couldn't
  electricians be delighted? Cowboys
  deranged? Models deposed?
  Dry cleaners depressed?

Where's The Beef?

"Inflation is getting out of hand!"
Margo complained to her best friend.
"Yesterday I went to a fancy restaurant
and ordered a forty dollar steak.
I told the waiter to put it on my
credit card—and it fit!"

I know not all
that may be coming,
but be it what it will,
I'll go to it laughing.

Herman Melville

Laugh and the world
laughs with you.

Ella Wheeler Wilcox

Always leave them
laughing when you say goodbye.

George Michael Cohan

Just For Fun!

The next time you're at the
mall with a friend, why not
try on a little laughter for size?
When your friend is looking
through a rack of clothing, head
to the opposite side of the rack.
Then, burst through the clothing
and shout, "Pick me! Pick me!"

*W*e have been
friends together in
sunshine and shade.

Caroline Norton

To everything there is a season,
and a time to every purpose under the heaven…
a time to weep, and a time to laugh;
a time to mourn, and a time to dance.

Ecclesiastes 3:1,4

*M*any friends will
walk in and out of your life,
but only true friends
will leave footprints
in your heart.

Eleanor Roosevelt

A little word in kindness spoken,
A motion or a tear,
Has often healed the heart that's broken,
And made a friend sincere.

Daniel Clement Colesworthy

Just For Laughs!

An elementary teacher was preparing to discuss magnetism with her class. She held a magnet over a box filled with pins and then said, "My name begins with 'm' and I pick up things. What am I?"

A girl in the front row immediately yelled out, "MOM!"

What sunshine is to flowers,
smiles are to humanity.
They are but trifles
to be sure;
but, scattered along
life's pathway,
the good they do
is inconceivable.

Joseph Addison

It is the heart that is not yet
sure of its God that is afraid
to laugh in His presence.

George MacDonald

Mistaken Identity

Once every year, three well-to-do sisters got together to catch up on their lives—and talk about what they'd sent their hard-to-please mother for her birthday.

"This year, I sent Mom a Mercedes AND a driver," the first said proudly.

The second said, "I can top that! I built her a new house!"

The eldest daughter said, with a confident smile, "I've got you both beat. You know how Mom enjoys reading Shakespeare, but can't see very well? I sent her a parrot that can recite the entire works of Shakespeare. It took hundreds of grad students over twelve years to teach him. I had to pledge $20,000 a year for 20 years to the university's *theater program to compensate them for their beloved mascot. But it's worth it!"*

Soon after, the daughters received their thank you notes.

To the first daughter, the mother wrote, "I'm too old to travel. I stay home all the time, so I never use the car—and the driver is rude."

To the second daughter she wrote, "The house is too big. I live in only one room and still have to clean all the rest."

To the eldest daughter she wrote, "Dearest, you're the only daughter to have the good sense to know what your mother likes. The chicken was delicious."

William Shakespeare
On Laughter

With mirth and laughter let old wrinkles come.
Merchant of Venice

Laugh yourselves into stitches.
Twelfth Night

If you tickle us do we not laugh?
Merchant of Venice

Grocery Store Giggles

Lauren was in the supermarket bright and early. As she pushed her cart down the cookie aisle, she saw a little girl begging her mother for cookies. When the girl's mother said, "No" the little girl began screaming at the top of her lungs.

In a quiet voice, the mother kept repeating, "Don't get excited, Monica. Don't scream, Monica. Don't be upset, Monica. Don't yell, Monica. Keep calm, Monica."

At the check-out counter Lauren wound up behind the young mother. She commented, "I couldn't help noticing how patient you were with little Monica!"

The woman replied, "I'm Monica!"

If instead of a gem,
or even a flower,
we should cast the
gift of a loving thought
into the heart of a friend,
that would be giving
as the angels give.

George McDonald

I can't imagine this
journey without someone
like you by my side.
You're like the chocolate chips
in the trail mix of my life.

*T*wo may talk together
under the same roof for
many years,
yet never really meet;
and two others
at first speech
are old friends.

Mary Catherwood

When the heart overflows
with gratitude or with any other sweet
and sacred sentiment,
what is the word to which it
would give utterance?
A friend.

Walter Savage Landor

*To get the full value
of joy, you must have
somebody to divide it with.*

Mark Twain

If we would build on a sure
foundation in friendship,
we must love our friends
for their sakes rather than for our own;
we must look at their truth to themselves
full as much as their truth to us.

Charlotte Bronte

Just For Fun!

Tired of your wardrobe, but finances too tight for a trip to the mall? Have a Castaway Party. Invite several friends to bring over any clothing or accessories they no longer wear and are willing to trade. Spend the evening "shopping" each other's castoffs.

If you want to carry the theme even further, have everyone bring along leftovers from the fridge. Swap, so everyone has a "new" dinner to take home with them.

Let's face it...

if you have melted chocolate on your hands, you're simply eating too slowly!

Remember the good old days when we were kids? Back then, all we had to do to lose weight was take a bath.

Just For Laughs!

One friend said to another, "My daughter seems to be getting a lot out of her college courses. She's very bright, you know. Every time we get an email from her, we have to take out the dictionary."

Her friend replied, "You're so lucky! Every time we hear from our daughter we have to take out a loan!"

Heavenly Home Run

Celia was devastated when she found out her best friend, Dorothy, was ill. Celia visited Dorothy in the hospital every day, where they laughed and relived memories from the years they'd shared together.

They reminisced about their winning seasons on the women's softball league in High School, then in college and later on with their church league. Celia jokingly told Dorothy that if there was a women's softball team in heaven she'd have something to look forward to. That night, Dorothy died.

Celia was awakened shortly afterward by a flash of light. She heard

Dorothy's voice calling to her out of the darkness, "Celia!" she heard her friend whisper, "I have good news and I have bad news!"

"Go ahead, Dorothy," Celia replied. "I can take it."

Dorothy's voice continued, "The good news is there IS a team! The bad news is you're pitching on Tuesday."

*Y*ears may wrinkle
the skin, but to give up
enthusiasm wrinkles
the soul.

Samuel Ullman

Happiness is not a state
to arrive at, but,
rather a manner of traveling.

Samuel Johnson

Is it so small a thing
to have enjoyed the sun,
to have light in the spring,
to have loved,
to have thought,
to have done?

Matthew Arnold

Spend all you have for loveliness,
Buy it and never count the cost...
And for a breath of ecstasy
Give all that you have been,
or could be.

Sara Teasdales

*A*lways I have a
chair for you in the
smallest parlor in
the world, to wit,
my heart.

Emily Dickinson

We are advertised by
our loving friends.

William Shakespeare

Humor is mankind's
greatest blessing.

Mark Twain

Road Trip

Three friends were driving down the highway at a very slow speed. A patrolman pulled them over and said that driving so slowly could be hazardous for other drivers.

The driver explained that she was following the posted limit: 20 miles per hour.

"M'am," the officer said, trying to hide a smile, "that sign indicates you are traveling on Highway 20."

"Well," the woman replied, "that explains why Lisa has been so quiet back there. Apparently we just turned off of Highway 125."

*S*ome people say
impulse shopping,
eating too much and
letting the housework
go is a symptom of aging,
depression and stress.
I call it "a perfect day."

*I*t's not how
old you are, but how
you are old.

Jules Renard

Always laugh when you can;
it is cheap medicine.
Merriment is a philosophy
not well understood.
It is the sunny side of existence.

Lord Byron

Mark Twain On Living Life to the Fullest

The two most important days in your life are the day you are born and the day you find out why.

The human race has one really effective weapon, and that is laughter.

Work like you don't need the money. Dance like no one is watching. And love like you've never been hurt.

A good and wholesome thing is a little harmless fun in this world.

Just For Laughs!

Friend: What did your husband get you for your birthday?

Birthday Girl: Well I asked him for something shiny that goes from zero to 150 in 3 seconds or less. So, now we're not speaking.

Friend: How come?

Birthday Girl: He gave me a bathroom scale.

A TRUE FRIEND
is someone who…

…remembers your birthday,
   but forgets your age.

…says nice things about you
   behind your back.

…will take your call, even if she's
   in the tub.

…only keeps a secret from you when
   she's planning your surprise party.

…knows everything about you,
   but loves you anyway.

A flower unblown; a book unread;
A tree with fruit unharvested;
A path untrod; a house whose rooms
Lack yet the heart's divine perfumes:
A landscape whose wide border lies
In silent shade, 'neath silent skies;
A treasure with its gifts concealed—
This is the year that for you waits
Beyond tomorrow's mystic gates.

Horatio Nelson Powers

The belief that youth
is the happiest time
of life is founded on fallacy.
The happiest person
is the person who thinks
the most interesting thoughts,
and we grow happier
as we grow older.

William Lyon Phelps

It is pleasing to the dear God
whenever thou rejoicest or laughest
from the bottom of thy heart.
Martin Luther

*L*et your boat of life
be light, packed only
with what you need—
a homely home and
simple pleasures, one or two
friends worth the name,
someone to love and
someone to love you.

Jerome K. Jerome

A Friend may well be reckoned
the masterpiece of Nature.

Ralph Waldo Emerson

I count myself in
nothing else so happy,
As in a soul rememb'ring
my good friends.

William Shakespeare

A good laugh is sunshine in a house.

William Makepeace Thackeray

We don't stop playing
because we grow old;
we grow old because
we stop playing.

George Bernard Shaw

Games to Play With Our Friends as We Age

- *Sag, You're It*
- *Hide and Go To Sleep*
- *Pin the Toupe on the Bald Guy*
- *Spin the Bottle (of Antacid)*
- *Musical Recliners*
- *Simon Says…Something Incoherent*

Friends Share Everything

Two elderly women who'd been friends for more than 70 years walked slowly into a fast food restaurant and ordered a single kids' meal. Settling themselves into a booth, they carefully cut the solitary burger in half and divided the small bag of fries, one-by-one, between them. Next, they took turns taking one sip of soda from the cup. Finally, one lady began slowly eating her half of the burger, while the other sat patiently, waiting her turn to eat.

Surmising the elderly women didn't have enough money to purchase meals of their own (and secretly hoping that when she grew older she'd enjoy as sweet a friendship as these two women seemed to share) a young woman offered to order them another meal.

The woman who was eating smiled and said, "Thank you, but we're fine." She continued chewing her half of the burger while her friend continued watching. Again, the young women felt compelled to offer her assistance. But once again, the elderly woman reassured her that they were just fine. They enjoyed sharing everything.

The young woman turned to the woman who hadn't started her meal yet and asked, "If you enjoy sharing everything so much, what are you waiting for?" "The teeth," the woman replied.

*T*he best mirror
is an old friend.

George Herbert

Laughter is a bodily exercise
precious to health.

Aristotle

Encouragement is oxygen
to the soul.

George M. Adams

A light heart lives long.

William Shakespeare

Humor is the great thing,
the saving thing. The minute it crops up,
all our irritations and resentments
slip away and a sunny spirit
takes their place.

Mark Twain

May God grant you always…
A sunbeam to warm you,
A moonbeam to charm you,
A sheltering Angel so nothing
can harm you.
Laughter to cheer you.
Faithful friends near you.
And when you pray,
For Heaven to hear you.

Irish Blessing